Map

of

the

Mind

Mark F. Kailing, PsyD

Map of the Mind

First published in 2016 by LaDena Kailing, Copyright ©
2016.

ISBN-13:978-1530356973

ISBN-10:1530356970

"This book is dedicated to my fellow philosophers, from whom humanity has been continually tutored. Much of my contribution is simply integrating their astounding discoveries. I also salute those precious few who continually seek truth no matter the cost— your courage gives humanity dignity and purpose, as well as hope."

-Dr. Mark Kailing

Foreward

Imagine you are sitting in a small lecture room listening to profound ideas about human nature and how to effectively strengthen every area of your life. These deep topics are taught in an environment of love and concern for you. They are explained so simply that you are able to come to your own conclusion about each subject quickly. That is what the Self Mastery Lecture Series is.

This book is one of several from the Self Mastery Lecture Series, transcribed from recordings taken in 2011. Mark Kailing battled cancer during that time, but continued his weekly lectures. Dr. Kailing was a Psychologist for 16 years serving clients in California, Nevada and Utah.

He loved to teach. During his education a professor taught him, "You don't truly understand something until you can explain it simply". This led Mark to develop simplified theories on life, personality, the Universe, truth, core fears and more. His ability to make the profound simple is what made him a great teacher and leader. Dr. Kailing lectured to thousands of students and clients over the years. He always lectured with a big smile on his face and spark in his eye. He was inspired by those who also desired to grow and improve in life.

Dr. Kailing passed away on May 21, 2013 after battling cancer for three and a half years. His example and influence have been felt by countless family, friends, clients, and colleagues. At the time of his death, he and LaDena had been married for 21 years and were raising their five children, Andrew (16), Aubrielle (15), Ammoriah (12), Ava (8) and Amari (4) in a home filled with adventures and love.

Reviews

"I have attended Mark's Self-Mastery lectures for over four months. His testimony, insights and philosophies have expanded my perspective and strengthened me so much it is difficult for me to express."

Tex Keen, Mendon, UT

"I was only able to attend one of Mark's lectures, but it changed a portion of my life forever."

Jenn Morris, Logan UT

"Simply put, Dr. Mark saved my life. Everyone should read these books. Not only read them, but really think about the magnitude of what is being said. Try to apply it in your life. The results will speak for themselves. I knew Mark and greatly miss our conversations. These books are his voice now...listen to him."

Curtis Bankhead, Logan, UT

"Mark's words are truly inspired! Each paragraph is so profound, I have learned so much! Thank you, thank you, thank you!!!"

Christopher Hostetter, Salt Lake City, UT

A message from LaDena Kailing:

I would encourage you to read this slowly. Take the time to ponder the messages you will read here. You may not agree with all that is shared, but stretch your mind to consider it. You will be glad you did. I've attended this lecture series, and have had deep conversations with Mark about these topics countless times. I'm still learning. I'm still finding little treasures of truth that help me feel excited about my own growth and influence in the world. I hope that happens for you too.

Thank you. I wish you all the best on your path.

We're going to talk about psychology, the history of psychology and the best of psychology.

I'd like to organize this lecture into kind of a history lesson. It's interesting what psychology has discovered. Psychology has been studied for around 100 years, thanks to Sigmund Freud. It's pretty interesting what the history reveals and why psychology was driven to discover what it discovered at each stage of history. Stay with me and you will see what I mean in just a minute.

If you like history like I do I think you'll enjoy the lecture today. We'll make this half a lesson in history and half a lesson in psychology.

Let's go back in time about a hundred years ago to Sigmund Freud, the father of modern psychology. You either love him or you hate him. He was a strange fellow, but a genius none the less. This was the Victorian Era with Queen Victoria on the throne, and she had a bit of a reputation of being a prude. That might be an understatement. She had such prudish rules, and everyone in England wanted to be just like the Queen. She is the style-setter. England had an empire spanning the globe and everyone wanted to be like the Queen of England. She is probably the reason you see the English walk tall and straight and they keep their buttocks tight while they walk. They would never break wind in public.

They view Americans as crass because we kind of let it all hang out, we'll burp, fart and scratch in public. The British are so prim and proper like Queen Victoria. Queen Victoria did not believe that women should enjoy sex. She said such things as, " Women should close their eyes, turn their head and do their Christian duty but they should not enjoy it." She was a strong woman and a great leader but she was strict in her belief about how people should behave. She believed that poor behavior could cheapen or discredit the monarchy.

This mentality put a lot of pressure on the people, teaching them that you had to pretend that you are perfect even though you are not. This places a lot of pressure on people which builds up and the people start to act a little nutty. When you repress these emotions too tightly for too long people go a little nutty.

In Queen Victoria's era the people resisted that nuttiness for so long but the pressure kept building up. The people developed hidden problems. There were problems of paralyzed limbs. The mind can build up such pressure, such guilt and insecurity about what you want to do with your hands like strangle someone or do sexual acts using your hands that the repressed feelings, which are unspeakable in their minds and in society, caused them to develop a paralyzed hand over the issue. They had a psychosomatic situation where your body is subconsciously telling you what you are feeling by expressing your pain in a physical way. People would wake up one morning and have a paralyzed limb. There was an epidemic of this. Sigmund Freud was a nerve doctor, a neurologist, who had recently graduated. No one had figured out the case of the paralyzed limbs because there was no scientific evidence, no brain injuries, no trauma, there were no spinal injuries. People speculated it might be evil spirits, and no scientist wanted to take on the case without scientific evidence.

Sigmund Freud was a new doctor and took whatever was given to him. He took on the case, and, as any scientist would do, he took himself out of the equation and observed naturally. He wanted to know what they were thinking and feeling so he had them lay down and he got out of their way, out of their vision, he sat behind them. He didn't know what he was doing but he simply said, "Say whatever comes to your mind, hold nothing back." Then he started writing.

That process, of having the patient say whatever came to mind without holding back was the invention of what we call psychoanalysis. This is the Freudian type of therapy that you see in the movies. At first, as you can imagine in the Victorian Era, people were nervous. They wondered what the proper thing to do was. Eventually they relaxed and started to say what it was that they were really feeling and thinking. Maybe they said they hated trying to always be prim and proper. Maybe they said they were sick of trying to be perfect all of the time. They start expressing their true human feelings. Pretty soon they started using their limb, the one that was paralyzed. Freud thought, "A-ha! I've cured you!"

He had no idea how he did it, so he came up with a theory to explain how he was curing the people.

Freud came up with a theory that basically a person had built up too much emotional pressure inside.

He was probably borrowing from a new invention at the time, the steam engine. A steam engine works when enough pressure has been built up that it forces something to move in order to relieve the pressure. He said that a human being is like a steam engine; if we build up enough emotional pressure inside ourselves, our needs, insecurities and fears build up, we will eventually be forced into a way of behaving that relieves the pressure. We will eventually do something nutty like punch our boss in the nose.

Freud developed this theory that said a healthy and wise human being should gradually relieve the pressure. We have to be a good parent, and look at our emotions as like a small child. Ask yourself everyday "What do my emotions need?" Then remind yourself that we need to take care of those needs gradually, moderately and safely before they build up and cause something extreme to happen in order to relieve the pressure.

Freud was accused of being an extremist but he wasn't. Many puritanical Christians of the time believed they should not admit their needs. Freud was telling the people that we all have needs and encouraging them to admit it, talk about it and then moderately relieve them. The people thought this was the devil's work encouraging people to relieve themselves sexually in a gradual, moderate way before they went out and possibly raped someone. Freud encouraged people to take their issues out on a punching bag instead of punching their boss.

This might be why it is healthy for men to play sports, so they let some aggression out in a gradual way. At the time, many people were afraid of this theory. What would happen to a seriously religious-based culture if they moderated their expectations? What a dangerous thing. What if they said, "All of these moral expectations that we have, we are going to cut them in half. We are going to ease up on our values."

That is a dangerous thing to say to people, especially teenagers. We have to be really careful with that. There was a lot of fear around this, and Freud probably got as many death threats as he did new clients. He became successful and left the hospital to set up a private practice and did extremely well. Freud's theory takes a look at the feelings of humans.

MAP OF THE MIND

The first theory in psychology takes a look at feelings.

Now, they that necessity is the mother of invention, when society needs something, that society is forced to invent what they need. People needed psychology badly. There were fears, insecurities and problems but the people were unsure if they wanted to go to a therapist and lay on a sofa in some old guy's living room while he sat behind them then he asked them to discuss their sexual fantasies. Most people that seek psychological help, it is the same then as it is today, are women. Women tend to seek internal knowledge more than men do. That means that there were young, wealthy women seeking psychological help but their fathers were uncomfortable with the process.

People wanted psychology but they wanted psychology that was safe, like it is when you go see a doctor in a hospital. Society wanted psychology to be more of a science. Psychology tried to create a purely scientific process. Scientists only work with what you can physically see, physical manifestations. You can't work on someone's feelings, they are a mess. There is nothing scientific in that. There was a decision for focus solely on the person's behavior. Behavior, like a rat in a maze, is measureable. You can state how many times the rat did this or that. You can formulate ideas about how to make the rat do this or that.

This brand of psychology, called Behaviorism, came around 1930.

These behaviorists helped people who saw them at the hospital. They looked at the behavior, for example a smoker. They then looked at scientific reasons that people smoked less. One of the things they discovered is that people tend to react according to rewards and punishments. People will behave more in ways that gain them rewards and will behave less in ways that provoke punishment. If you look carefully at your own life, we will tend to do misbehaviors as long as we are getting away with it. We do them until we are caught, punished and experience the consequences. Sometimes there are serious misbehaviors and at times these people are glad they got caught. There have been serial killers who have stated that they were glad it is finally over so they can be punished and stop the behavior. In history at this time there was the use of electricity. Inventions were being made that replaced man-power with electricity and this was exciting for society.

Behaviorists found a way to use electricity in psychology, as a punishment for poor behaviors. They figured they should hook up the electricity to whatever part of the body they were misusing; if they were an overeater they hooked up the tongue, if they were a sexual perpetrator they hooked up their genitalia. They had a machine that could tell if there was swelling in the genitalia after the subject looked at certain pictures. If they became aroused they got zapped. A lot of people did not volunteer for this type of therapy. It became very popular to use in prisons and psych hospitals, this was before patient rights. These patients had no choice.

Back then, doctors were considered godlike.

People listened to their doctor's orders. We don't respect doctors today like we did back then. Psychologists at this time were kind of extremists. They viewed humans as animal-like who can be trained with rewards and punishments. Rewards and punishments have been shaping us since we were born. When a child burns his hand on the hot stove, he will then be afraid and cautious around the stove, he won't do it again. This system has shaped all of us more than we can imagine. I don't think this is the only factor that has shaped us, but it is certainly one of them.

What was going on in history at the time that promoted this kind of philosophy? People were building empires. This was before the time of the Second World War. People thought that "Might made right". People who were strong enough to inflict the rewards and punishment were the ones who should be in control. When you hear about mad scientists, in the movies and such it was from this era. The United States, as well as Hitler, had programs where they would try and use rewards and punishments to control people to an extreme degree.

Necessity is the mother of invention and it was time for change. There were still a lot of mental health problems but people did not want to seek help from psychoanalysis or behaviorist processes.

In the 1950s we came up with another kind of therapy, something that was more comfortable for the client.

To find something more neutral, away from the hospital and from the doctor's living room, doctors chose to meet clients in an office instead. At the office the client didn't lay down on a bed, or on an operating table, but they sat in a comfortable chair. The doctor didn't wear a white coat but wore a business suit and a tie. This is like our modern therapists. These doctors did not want to process feelings, they wanted to look at logic.

Logic is a very clean thing, no messy feelings. You might guess that psychology is a very male-dominated field and men wanted to process logic not emotions. Women were not in the work-force yet, they were in the homes. So there was a theory that just focused on thoughts and logic. After meeting with the doctor, he would then tell the patient how to think and act logically.

The problem with this therapy is that it was prejudiced. Not only were the therapists male but they were white, upper class, American males. This therapy was culturally insensitive. They were basically trying to teach clients how to be like them. It's dangerous to give that much power to one culture who state that they are superior to all other cultures.

This was the 50s, what was going on in history at the time? We had invented the atom bomb and empire building became too dangerous. It could end life on the planet, so we developed a new type of war, a cold war. A cold war is a war of propaganda, where each side tried to get the other to think like they did. America developed the great talent of taking over countries by putting in leaders in those countries who thought like us. To be more specific, those who thought like the American, upper class, white males. The cold war began and therapists were influenced by the American arrogance.

At the time we were taught to believe that America was a superpower, and the only problem with the rest of the world is that they are not American. It was a comfortable type of therapy. It was easier for the public to accept than previous types of therapy, but it lacked the respect for other ways of thinking and behaving. Another type of pressure built up and we needed to develop another type of therapy. What took place over the next twenty years were two wars that people felt really bad about. In Korea and Vietnam people were constantly fighting over political ideas. After our thinking matured, we didn't feel that the fight was worth the cost of all of those lives in order to change another country's belief system.

The people got sick of this kind of warfare. During John F. Kennedy's presidency there was the Bay of Pigs in Cuba, and there was the possibility that the world could've been annihilated with nuclear weapons because Cuba wanted to become communist. People got sick of the American arrogance. Some of this still lingers. We shouldn't be embarrassed about this, we are still maturing. We wanted a new type of therapy that promoted peace not war. People wanted a therapy that had respect of all cultures as being equally valuable.

The hippie movement was fueled by this frustration with American arrogance.

The hippie movement basically said that everyone's philosophies are equally valid. There is some truth to that statement. Never think that one truth is the only truth. History is replete with problems from thinking that we have found the one truth. Every truth has an opposite truth. We need to bring balance to the equation.

We should respect all philosophies, but are they all equally valid in every single situation? No. It is a lovely thought but it's not always practical. Hippies discovered that as they did whatever they wanted in every situation that there were times they should restrain themselves. Sometimes an idea is not good in a particular situation. Having a commune of 100 people, where everyone had free sex, eventually proved itself to not be a good system. This era was fueled by following our feelings. This is where we got the phrases, "Just follow your heart" and "If it feels good, do it". This led to a lot of fluffy, feel-good solutions that were short-sided.

Sometimes doing what makes us most happy is not the best thing for us, our children, your job or our society. It's not realistic. A type of therapy was inspired by the hippy movement. It did not want to blame anybody for a mistake. Blaming someone was akin to saying "your philosophy is not good, you were wrong." We wanted a philosophy that stated that no one was every guilty, and no one was ever wrong. So what happened when there was a problem? We didn't want to blame a person, so we chose to blame the environment.

Essentially, this is 'a blame the environment' philosophy.

You might have heard the old saying, "We're all just a product of our environment." This was a 1970s movement. It stated that if we all had an ideal environment, plenty of love, resources, and money, we would all be good people. We would all be really high-functioning, ideal human beings. If there are enough government programs to help people out, paying money for their problems and solving their problems for them, everyone would be great.

The problem with that thinking is that it is only half true, it has an opposite truth like everything else. Everything should be in moderation. If you give everybody all the love, money and resources that they want they become spoiled. Eventually we have to take responsibility for our actions and our needs. This theory of blaming the environment was very addictive.

If you look closely, our world is still heavily influenced by this theory. I have parents calling me about their child's bad behavior and they cannot accept the responsibility that their parenting may have had something to do with it. People don't want to take blame for their problems. Blame is something that we are all afraid of so we have a black or white extreme reaction to it. Blame just means that we are imperfect. We are all imperfect therefore we all have blame. The right amount of blame can be quite motivating. How can we change something that we haven't admitted is a problem?

When I'm working with families, I'm not looking for one person to place the blame. The first thing I say to families or couples that come into my office is "Look, we are all imperfect and we are all going to share a part of the blame here. We are going to share equally so that no one has more than the other. We all could've done something better. Let's be productive and find out what that is. What can we do that is better?"

I highly recommend this to couples by the way. This is a great way to keep a peaceful marriage. When problems arise admit that each partner will split the blame equally knowing they both could've done some things better, then talk about what each can do to improve. Be very careful not to blame too much on one side or the other or the fight will continue. These therapists were fun to go to because when you went into their office they would tell you, "None of this is your fault, you poor dear. If only everyone understood you they would see how great you really are. They are the ones with the problems."

The therapist liked it because they got to be the hero by making the parents look bad. This therapy was not very good at accountability. Clients became lazy with this therapy. If something difficult in their lives needed to be changed, they didn't do the work to change it. The clients thought, "Why should I change? I don't feel like it."

The hippie movement got really messy with people doing whatever they felt like doing. By the way, one of the problems we are still facing today came from this philosophy, and that is our government heading toward bankruptcy. We've had a philosophy that if we have a problem, the government should throw money at it. If you look at this you'll see this is what bankrupts a government.

It would be interesting to see how many people have thought, at some point in their lives when they had a problem, "The government should throw money at this problem and fix it." It's as if there exists the expectation that the government has an endless supply of money. If you have to borrow money to fix a problem then you have another problem. If we had endless amounts of money, we could legitimately use that money to fix all kinds of problems.

This philosophy came from the idea that people should not suffer. Suffering is bad. Being a moderate myself, I think we need to look at both sides of that idea. A moderate amount of suffering is probably good. A moderate amount of suffering kicks us in the butt. It is motivating for us. People are usually at their best when they are under a little pressure. If you take all of the suffering out, you have an unmotivated society.

People got tired of the hippie movement, it rapidly increased the divorce rate, sexually transmitted diseases, babies born out of wedlock and a lot of relationship problems that come from sleeping from people you should not have slept with. People realized that this philosophy was creating a messy society. We wanted something that was more responsible, we didn't want to continue the philosophy that people could do whatever they wanted to, however we are not yet ready to blame ourselves. We want to blame something other than the environment so we decided to blame our body chemistry.

Now we are at the 1980s and the invention of Prozac and many more psychological medicines.

This movement was similar to the hippie movement in that we wanted to blame something other than ourselves so we blamed our biology. At this time if anybody had a problem you would hear them say they had a chemical imbalance. Society wanted a quick fix pill for everything.

I'll tell you a story, I recently had surgery and I experienced first-hand that when you take a pill for something it creates side effects and then you need a pill to compensate for the side effects. Pretty soon the doctors were giving me so many pills it was overwhelming. It took my body two weeks to stop the nausea from all of the chemicals from the pills I was taking. That was crazy. Now, again, I'm a moderate and I'm not saying that medications are bad, we just need to see a more realistic, moderate view on them. We don't need a medication to fix every tiny little symptom. Take the medication when it becomes necessary, when we are really hurting and after we've tried other forms of healing.

If we take a pill for every little thing, pretty soon every human being is on twenty different medications and we're not entirely sure how all medications react with one another. If you read online about each of these psychological medications you will see that we kind of understand how they work but we don't have a lot long-term research on these drugs so we're not entirely sure what will happen over time. You will see commercials about lawyers seeking additional clients who have taken some of these drugs and suffered problems because of them.

Let's be wise. Everything should be in moderation. The body chemistry issue is real and people do benefit from medicines, but be careful to do it moderately.

What is the consequence of all of this? It's still a little early to know, but the rates of cancer and other illnesses are rapidly increasing. This has been since we've become enamored with body chemistry we thought we could just throw chemicals at every problem. If you read the ingredients of most of the products that we buy in the grocery store, you cannot pronounce most of the ingredients. If you buy microwaveable popcorn the ingredients should be butter and popcorn, right? Instead you will find a long list of unpronounceable things. What is the consequence to this obsession with chemicals? Many health problems are on the rise as well as new health issues such as fibromyalgia.

Now we are in the 1990s, when I was going to school for school to be a psychologist, it was a weird time to be studying psychology.

We were required to study all of this history as psychology students, but each professor had grown up in their own school of thought and they were very prejudiced against the other ones. As a student you had to learn all of the therapies but if the professor discovered you favored one different from the one that they did, they gave you a lower grade.   The students kept quiet about which theory that we liked best.

I challenged a professor once, I was into Freud's teachings and he was into behaviorism and I challenged him on a paper. I thought it would be interesting and that the professor would like an intellectual debate. Wrong! He gave me a big old F. The students would whisper in the hallways to ask, "Which theory do you like best?" Finally, there was a growing movement toward the end of my schooling where you could like all of them. They all work.   Some worked better for some type of problems and some worked better for other type of problems. Some worked better for one type of person, and some worked better for another type of person.

Research showed that they all worked so what would be wrong with liking all of them then? We started the word 'eclectic'. Eclectic means that you like it all. I had a brilliant eclectic professor tell us, after the class asked which type of therapy we should use on a certain case, "It depends on which point of entry you would like to use into the clients system. These words were music to my ears.

Each therapy was just a different point of entry into a human being; their thoughts, their moods, their behaviors, their biology and their environment. It's like an engine with all of the parts working together in a system. It doesn't matter which one you choose. If it's a system, and you change one, you'll change all of them. It's like all of these things fit in a circle and it flows around and around. When you change one, it will cause a change in the others.

Eclectic therapy was very demanding for psychologists for them to be so broadly trained but it was worth it though. We figured all of these theories fit together in some kind of system but we didn't have an idea of how it worked. This, my friends, is what I think is the best way to put this all together.

Whatever happens to us from our environment, first triggers a feeling. Feelings are triggered quicker than logic. If something falls on your head, the first feeling will be a pain reaction before you logically figure out what it is. The idea is that our logic, our thinking, has evolved to solve our feelings. Animals had feelings long before they had thoughts. Our thoughts are to help us solve emotion. Proof of that is, the stronger your feelings are, the faster your thinking is. If you have mild feelings, then your thoughts are like, "Well, I'll get around to that. Whatever, I don't know." If you have strong feelings about something, your mind races into action trying to figure it the feeling. It's like feelings are the accelerator that trigger the logic.

Next, whatever thought you come up with will depict your behavior. It's like a circle, feelings trigger thoughts, thoughts trigger behaviors. Whatever thoughts you have will influence how you behave. I'll give you an example; say a brick fell off a building and hit me in the head. I look up and see a man on the roof. I could think that the man threw the brick on purpose, or that man saw what happened and he is checking on me to see if I'm alright. You can be very sure that my behavior will be different depending upon which thought I come up with.

It's very important that each of us become a good logician in this world because however good your thinking is will determine how good of a life you have. It will affect how good your behavior is. It will determine how effective your behavior is in any given situation. If you have poor logic, you will have poor behaviors that don't work. Poor behaviors will cause some problems in your environment, others may become angry with you or you could behave in ways that cause harm to your body, mind and spirit. Coming around the circle your behavior influences your environment. The environment will treat you according to how you behave.

What if you have to solve a challenging problem and you have intense feelings about it, how do you go about making a good, healthy choices to solve the problem?

The best way to do that according to modern psychology is to look at this circle of different psychological therapies and choose which one of these would be the easiest for you to change for you as an individual and for that situation? This answer will change according to individuals and according to the situation. Say for example that I'm locked in jail. I'm not able to change my environment anytime soon, that situation has taken that option away from me. I'm not able to improve my environment by taking a hot bath or burning some incense.

If I'm not a very logical person, then changing my thinking is probably not the easiest way to improve my situation. If I'm a very impulsive person, then changing my behaviors will be very difficult for me and I should probably choose a different one. I'm very good at meditation so for me I would prefer to make sure that I'm calm first. I wouldn't do anything until my body was calm. I help many of my clients proceed by giving them training in how to be calm in any given situation. If it was a problem at work, if you are able to remain calm you will be able to think more clearly, behave better, your body chemistry will be more balanced, and people will respond more favorably to you. That is where I always start personally and I've taught many of my clients this. It depends on the situation and the person.

Emotions are like an inner child and logic is like the inner parent. Does a parent make all decisions without regard to the child's feelings? No, the parent has to listen to the child's needs, and at the same time, do what is logical. So, you have to listen to your feelings and listen to your logic. Some people are good at logic, some people are good at feelings. You really need a balance of both. It's a classic question, "Should I follow my head or my heart?" Everybody who has ever been in love has had that question! You will be safest betting on two horses rather than one, you should listen to both.

This circle of psychological therapies each leading into the other; feelings to thoughts, thoughts to behaviors, behaviors to environment and then biology is in the center of the circle. Biology, like the hub of the wheel affects all of them. This is the best diagram we have of how a human being works. I have to convey to you how important this diagram really is. It took humans all of these years, to come up with this map of a human being. This is extremely powerful.

You can diagram any problem by plugging in the particulars. If you have a friend who is contemplating a divorce, ask what is going on with their biology is that is affecting the problem. What is going on with their thinking, with their feelings and with their environment. This psychological wheel goes around and around and you can keep going back in time for all of the factors that have influenced this problem.

You could be a wise psychologist and put me out of business just by using this psychological theories wheel, this map of how humans work. You could be sitting with a friend at a restaurant and they lay their problem on you and you get out a napkin and write down this diagram. Ask your friend what the problem is and perhaps they said, "My husband sucks." You could teach them that this is their environment and now they can work backwards ask what the husband is behaving like and she might say something like, "He leaves the toilet seat up every time".

Next, ask about her thinking and why it bothers her so much and she might say, "Well, because I take that as a sign of disrespect that he would leave the toilet seat up". You can ask her why she takes that as a sign of disrespect and she might say, "It feels like he doesn't love me when he does that." I know this is a silly example and pardon me for being so silly. You can ask the friend why it makes her feel unloved and she could say that "Lately, I don't feel loved. He forgot our anniversary, he works late all of the time and then when he's home he is watching TV then goes to bed."

Now, you are getting to the bottom of the problem. She isn't feeling enough love energy from him lately and that is what is making the toilet seat issue a bigger deal than it would be otherwise. If she felt plenty of love coming from him the toilet seat would be a small issue.

I wish I could say that all psychologists know this circle diagram of the eclectic psychological therapies, and that all psychologists are good at this process but they do not. Most psychologists don't know this information and they don't use it. It is an extremely valuable thing to use to assess a situation. In my school there was a lot of broad training and I'm naturally interesting in almost everything so I studied all of these theories in college. I liked them all so I had to find a way to put them together. This is where psychology should be. This circle is so important about our human race. It's like a map of what makes us tick, what life is like as a human being. What affects us. If this diagram fell into the wrong hands it would be an extremely dangerous tool.

Let's talk about the future. What is the future of psychology?

We are just tapping into that right now. It is happening already. It is an early movement and it focuses on energy. If you think about what is really going on in the modern world it is energy that is the most important issue. We keep trying to discover an unlimited, renewable source of energy by splitting atoms, cold fusion, or hot fusion. Whoever discovers an unlimited source of energy will change the world.

Interestingly to look at, all of our problems as a culture, as a society, come from competing over energy. We're like kids on a playground, "That's my cookie!" We compete over various forms of energy. Everything in the whole universe is made of energy, we are a sea of energy. We are competing over some type of energy; love, comfort, glory, power, or resources. If we found an unlimited source of energy, and I believe we are close, what would we have to compete over?

We need physical energy to power our machines but we also need energy in the form of love. We need spiritual energy. Those are already unlimited, we've already discovered the unlimited sources of those.

The universe already has an unlimited source of love if we learn to get fear and defenses out of our way so we can channel it. Like the example of that couple that was fighting over the toilet seat lid it was really an argument over energy, over love. If that woman had enough love energy from her husband she wouldn't be upset over that toilet seat.

You can really understand an argument at a deep level if you can see it terms of energy. What is the core of the issue? People often use drugs so that they can feel plenty of love energy. We all want it. We all want love, comfort, power, glory and other forms of energy. We can understand the core of everything if we see it in terms of energy. How does energy fit into the circle diagram?

Everything is made of energy, our thoughts, our behaviors, our environment, our body chemistry, all of it. Energy would be this ethereal cloud over all of it. It encompasses everything.

When someone comes to see me in therapy, this is why I try to help them to take in energy in the form of comfort. If you get really good at being able to provide yourself with comfort; smelling the flowers as you go, feeling the sun on your face, enjoying the beauty in the colors of nature in your eyes you can bring in these comforts, these energies. You can use mediation to channel energy. You will feel that you have plenty of energy in your life. Everything else will seem small by comparison, like a toilet seat was left up. It is very important to practice meditating to bring comfort to yourself; love, self-esteem, and peace.

Take in from the abundance of energy of the universe. There is plenty of it as soon as you learn to open the valves of your own body. Notice it around you; you are already swimming in comfort energy. This type of therapy is very powerful. Most people are getting excited about it. It's a new language to people, it might sound a little weird at first. It doesn't sound very scientific.

One mission that I feel is really important is to come up with a name for this theory that is palatable, something that feels normal. I get a little disappointed with my holistic colleagues that come up with funky names for this work such as "The Fifth Star of Omega Five, or Kundalini Energy" and many other unusual examples. When we focus on the cultural weirdness it will alienate four out of five people that come across it.

If you put in a neutral language like the word energy it resonates with most people, scientists and spiritualists alike. When I speak with my clients I try to use neutral language as I teach them how to take more energy in. I teach them how to enjoy life by experiencing more energy. We channel energy naturally when we eat, drink, walk, talk, and think. It's just a matter of taking the next step and asking, "How can I channel energy even better?"

I think the first step is to be more conscious of all of this. Think in terms of energy, "What is the energy doing?" This is very useful in relationships. People are more affected by your energy than they are by your looks, your behavior, or your words. They are affected more by the energy that you radiate. If you have really good energy, people will want to be around you.

The history of psychology has been very interesting. Where is the future going? What will happen after we master the energy theory? Who knows, but it will be exciting. You have to learn things step by step so let's master all of these things, let's analyze them and live them and then we will be prepared as a society to take the next step. It will be very exciting.

The other books in Mark Kailing's Self-Mastery Lecture Series:

Purpose of Life

Law of Integration

Dark Side of Relationships

The Gender War

Deeper Relationships

Battling our Core Fears

A Profoundly Open Mind

Lifelong Path of Grace

What We Now Know

Improve your Mental Health by Improving your Physical Health

Self-Mastery and Religion

Your Spiritual Path

Overcome your Core Fears

www.ingramcontent.com/pod-product-compliance
Lightning Source LLC
Chambersburg PA
CBHW071315280526
45788CB00004B/1899